"... With men this is impossible; but with God all things are possible."

–Matthew 19:26

What God Does Reveals What He Is.

-MIKE MURDOCK

2

"Verily, verily, I say unto you, He that believeth on Me, the works that I do shall he do also; and greater works than these shall he do; because I go unto My Father."

–John 14:12

When You Open Your Hands, God Will Open His Windows.

-MIKE MURDOCK

3

"And whatsoever ye shall ask in My name, that will I do, that the Father may be glorified in the Son."

–John 14:13

Uncommon Obedience Unleashes Uncommon Favor.

-MIKE MURDOCK

4

"For the Father loveth the Son, and sheweth Him all things that Himself doeth: and He will shew Him greater works than these, that ye may marvel. For as the Father raiseth up the dead, and quickeneth them; even so the Son quickeneth whom He will."

—John 5:20,21

When You Ask God For A Miracle He Will Give You An Instruction. *-MIKE MURDOCK*

5

"Jesus Christ the same yesterday, and to day, and for ever."

–Hebrews 13:8

Your Present Focus Determines Your Present Joy.

-MIKE MURDOCK

6

"Ye are of God, little children, and have overcome them: because greater is He that is in you, than he that is in the world."

-1 John 4:4

Warfare Always Surrounds The Birth Of A Miracle.

-MIKE MURDOCK

7

"For verily I say unto you, That whosoever shall say unto this mountain, Be thou removed, and be thou cast into the sea; and shall not doubt in his heart, but shall believe that those things which he saith shall come to pass; he shall have whatsoever he saith."

–Mark 11:23

Miracles Happen As Quickly As Tragedies.

-MIKE MURDOCK

8

"Therefore I say unto you, What things soever ye desire, when ye pray, believe that ye receive them, and ye shall have them."

–Mark 11:24

The Clearer Your Goal, The Greater Your Faith.

-MIKE MURDOCK

9

"So shall My Word be that goeth forth out of My mouth: it shall not return unto Me void, but it shall accomplish that which I please, and it shall prosper in the thing whereto I sent it."

-Isaiah 55:11

The Instruction You Follow Determines The Future You Create. -MIKE MURDOCK

10

"And when He had called unto Him His twelve disciples, He gave them power against unclean spirits, to cast them out, and to heal all manner of sickness and all manner of disease."

–Matthew 10:1

You Are Never As Far From A Miracle As It First Appears.

-MIKE MURDOCK

11

"And as ye go, preach, saying, The kingdom of heaven is at hand. Heal the sick, cleanse the lepers, raise the dead, cast out devils: freely ye have received, freely give."

–Matthew 10:7,8

What You Make Happen For Others, God Will Make Happen For You.

-MIKE MURDOCK

12

"If ye abide in Me, and My words abide in you, ye shall ask what ye will, and it shall be done unto you."

—John 15:7

Something God Has Given You Will Create Anything Else God Has Promised You.

-MIKE MURDOCK

13

"Trust in the Lord with all thine heart; and lean not unto thine own understanding."

-Proverbs 3:5

Someone You Are Believing Is Deciding What You Are Becoming.

-MIKE MURDOCK

14

"Jesus said unto him, If thou canst believe, all things are possible to him that believeth."

-Mark 9:23

One Day Of Favor Is Worth A Thousand Days Of Labor.

-MIKE MURDOCK

15

"Be still, and know that I am God: I will be exalted among the heathen, I will be exalted in the earth."

—Psalm 46:10

The Person Of Jesus Creates Your Peace—The Principles Of Jesus Create Your Prosperity.

—MIKE MURDOCK

16

"Now faith is the substance of things hoped for, the evidence of things not seen."

—Hebrews 11:1

Faith Is Simply Your Confidence In God.

—MIKE MURDOCK

17

"Who through faith subdued kingdoms, wrought righteousness, obtained promises, stopped the mouths of lions, Quenched the violence of fire, escaped the edge of the sword, out of weakness were made strong, waxed valiant in fight, turned to flight the armies of the aliens."

-Hebrews 11:33,34

Opposition Is Proof Of Progress.
-MIKE MURDOCK

18

"Behold, I give unto you power to tread on serpents and scorpions, and over all the power of the enemy: and nothing shall by any means hurt you."

–Luke 10:19

The Anointing You Respect Is The Anointing That Increases In Your Life.

-MIKE MURDOCK

19

"For since the beginning of the world men have not heard, nor perceived by the ear, neither hath the eye seen, O God, beside Thee, what He hath prepared for him that waiteth for Him."

-Isaiah 64:4

Passion Enables You To Find The Shortest Distance To Any Goal. *-MIKE MURDOCK*

20

"But seek ye first the kingdom of God, and His righteousness; and all these things shall be added unto you."

–Matthew 6:33

What You Do First Determines What God Will Do Next.

-MIKE MURDOCK

21

"Ye men of Israel, hear these words; Jesus of Nazareth, a man approved of God among you by miracles and wonders and signs, which God did by Him in the midst of you, as ye yourselves also know:"

–Acts 2:22

The Price God Was Willing To Pay Reveals The Worth Of The Product He Saw. *-MIKE MURDOCK*

22

"And these signs shall follow them that believe; In My name shall they cast out devils; they shall speak with new tongues; They shall take up serpents; and if they drink any deadly thing, it shall not hurt them; they shall lay hands on the sick, and they shall recover."

–Mark 16:17,18

What You Believe Determines What You Overcome.

-MIKE MURDOCK

23

"Jesus answered them, I told you, and ye believed not: the works that I do in My Father's name, they bear witness of Me."

–John 10:25

God's Only Pain Is To Be Doubted; God's Only Pleasure Is To Be Believed.

-MIKE MURDOCK

24

"How God anointed Jesus of Nazareth with the Holy Ghost and with power: Who went about doing good, and healing all that were oppressed of the devil; for God was with Him."

—Acts 10:38

The Anointed Are The Deliverers.

—MIKE MURDOCK

25

"And Jesus said unto them, Because of your unbelief: for verily I say unto you, If ye have faith as a grain of mustard seed, ye shall say unto this mountain, Remove hence to yonder place; and it shall remove; and nothing shall be impossible unto you."

-Matthew 17:20

The Seasons Of Your Life Will Change Every Time You Decide To Use Your Faith. *-MIKE MURDOCK*

26

"Behold, the Lord's hand is not shortened, that it cannot save; neither His ear heavy, that it cannot hear:"

-Isaiah 59:1

The Willingness To Reach Qualifies You To Receive.

-MIKE MURDOCK

27

"Jesus saith unto her, Said I not unto thee, that, if thou wouldest believe, thou shouldest see the glory of God?"

-John 11:40

God Never Responds To Pain—
God Only Responds To Faith.

-MIKE MURDOCK

28

"The great temptations which thine eyes saw, and the signs, and the wonders, and the mighty hand, and the stretched out arm, whereby the Lord thy God brought thee out: so shall the Lord thy God do unto all the people of whom thou art afraid."

–Deuteronomy 7:19

True Friends Have The Same Enemies.

-MIKE MURDOCK

29

"How great are His signs! and how mighty are His wonders! His kingdom is an everlasting kingdom, and His dominion is from generation to generation."

–Daniel 4:3

When You Get Involved With God's Dream, He Will Get Involved In Your Dream.

-MIKE MURDOCK

"...The Mighty God, the Lord of hosts, is His name, Great in counsel, and mighty in work: for Thine eyes are open upon all the ways of the sons of men: to give every one according to his ways, and according to the fruit of his doings: Which hast set signs and wonders in the land of Egypt, even unto this day, and in Israel, and among other men; and hast made thee a name, as at this day;"

–Jeremiah 32:18-20

If God Is Your Partner You Can Afford To Make Big Plans.

-MIKE MURDOCK

31

"So then faith cometh by hearing, and hearing by the Word of God."

−Romans 10:17

What Enters You Determines What Exits You.

-MIKE MURDOCK

DECISION

Will You Accept Jesus As Your Personal Savior Today?

The Bible says, "That if thou shalt confess with thy mouth the Lord Jesus, and shalt believe in thine heart that God hath raised Him from the dead, thou shalt be saved" (Romans 10:9).

Pray this prayer from your heart today!

"Dear Jesus, I believe that You died for me and rose again on the third day. I confess I am a sinner...I need Your love and forgiveness...Come into my heart. Forgive my sins. I receive Your eternal life. Confirm Your love by giving me peace, joy and supernatural love for others. Amen."

☐ Yes, Mike! I made a decision to accept Christ as my personal Savior today. Please send me my free gift of your book *"31 Keys to a New Beginning"* to help me with my new life in Christ. *(B-48)*

NAME _____

ADDRESS _____

CITY _____ STATE _____ ZIP _____

PHONE (____) _____ EMAIL _____

(B-208)

Mail To: **The Wisdom Center**
P.O. Box 99 · Denton, TX 76202
1-888-WISDOM-1 (1-888-947-3661)
Website: thewisdomcenter.tv

Unless otherwise indicated, all Scripture quotations are taken from the King James Version of the Bible.
Memory Bible On Miracles · ISBN 1-56394-277-1/B-208
Copyright © 2003 by **MIKE MURDOCK**
All publishing rights belong exclusively to Wisdom International
Published by The Wisdom Center · P.O. Box 99 · Denton, Texas 76202
1-888-WISDOM-1 (1-888-947-3661) · **Website: thewisdomcenter.tv**
11030100k

Financial Success.

- ▶ 8 Scriptural Reasons You Should Pursue Financial Prosperity

- ▶ The Secret Prayer Key You Need When Making A Financial Request To God

- ▶ The Weapon Of Expectation And The 5 Miracles It Unlocks

- ▶ How To Discern Those Who Qualify To Receive Your Financial Assistance

- ▶ How To Predict The Miracle Moment God Will Schedule Your Financial Breakthrough

- ▶ Habits Of Uncommon Achievers

- ▶ The Greatest Success Law I Ever Discovered

- ▶ How To Discern Your Place Of Assignment, The Only Place Financial Provision Is Guaranteed

- ▶ 3 Secret Keys In Solving Problems For Others

The Wisdom Center

Video Pak
AMVIDEO | $30
Buy 1-Get 1 Free
(A $60 Value!)

Wisdom Is The Principal Thing

Add 10% For S/H

Songs From The Secret Place!

The Music Ministry of MIKE MURDOCK

The Wisdom Center

6 Tapes | $30
PAK-007
Wisdom Is The Principal Thing

Free Book
B-100 ($10 Value)
ENCLOSED!
Wisdom Is The Principal Thing

Songs...

1. A Holy Place
2. Anything You Want
3. Everything Comes From You
4. Fill This Place With Your Presence
5. First Thing Every Morning
6. Holy Spirit, I Want To Hear You
7. Holy Spirit, Move Again
8. Holy Spirit, You Are Enough
9. I Don't Know What I Would Do Without You
10. I Let Go (Of Anything That Stops Me)
11. I'll Just Fall On You
12. I Love You, Holy Spirit
13. I'm Building My Life Around You
14. I'm Giving Myself To You
15. I'm In Love! I'm In Love!
16. I Need Water (Holy Spirit, You're My Well)

17. In The Secret Place
18. In Your Presence, I'm Always Changed
19. In Your Presence (Miracles Are Born)
20. I've Got To Live In Your Presence
21. I Want To Hear Your Voice
22. I Will Do Things Your Way
23. Just One Day At A Time
24. Meet Me In The Secret Place
25. More Than Ever Before
26. Nobody Else Does What You Do
27. No No Walls!
28. Nothing Else Matters Anymore (Since I've Been In The Presence Of You Lord)
29. Nowhere Else
30. Once Again You've Answered
31. Only A Fool Would Try (To Live Without You)

32. Take Me Now
33. Teach Me How To Please You
34. There's No Place I'd Rather Be
35. Thy Word Is All That Matters
36. When I Get In Your Presence
37. You're The Best Thing (That's Ever Happened To Me)
38. You Are Wonderful
39. You've Done It Once
40. You Keep Changing Me
41. You Satisfy

Add 10% For S/H

D THE WISDOM CENTER
P.O. Box 99, Denton, Texas 76202
1-888-WISDOM1
(1-888-947-3661)
Website:
WWW.THEWISDOMCENTER.TV

The *Uncommon* Woman

- ▸ **Master Keys In Understanding The Man In Your Life**
- ▸ **The One Thing Every Man Attempts To Move Away From**
- ▸ **The Dominant Difference Between A Wrong Woman And A Right Woman**
- ▸ **What Causes Men To Withdraw**

MIKE MURDOCK

THIRTY - ONE SECRETS of an UNFORGETTABLE WOMAN

MIKE MURDOCK

THE WISDOM FOR WOMEN SERIES

Master Secrets from the Life of Ruth

THE PROVERBS 31 Woman

MIKE MURDOCK

MENTORSHIP PROGRAM OF WISDOM

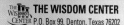

THE WISDOM CENTER
MIKE MURDOCK • P.O. Box 99 • Denton, Texas

31 Secrets of an Unforgettable Woman

The Wisdom Center

6 Tapes | $30
PAK-009
Wisdom Is The Principal Thing

Free Book Enclosed!
Wisdom Is The Principal Thing

My Gift Of Appreciation...

The Wisdom Commentary

The Wisdom Commentary includes 52 topics...for mentoring your family every week of the year.

These topics include:

- Abilities
- Achievement
- Anointing
- Assignment
- Bitterness
- Blessing
- Career
- Change
- Children
- Dating
- Depression
- Discipline
- Divorce
- Dreams And Goals
- Enemy
- Enthusiasm
- Favor
- Finances
- Fools

- Giving
- Goal-Setting
- God
- Happiness
- Holy Spirit
- Ideas
- Intercession
- Jobs
- Loneliness
- Love
- Mentorship
- Ministers
- Miracles
- Mistakes
- Money
- Negotiation
- Prayer
- Problem-Solving
- Protégés

- Satan
- Secret Place
- Seed-Faith
- Self-Confidence
- Struggle
- Success
- Time-Management
- Understanding
- Victory
- Weaknesses
- Wisdom
- Word Of God
- Words
- Work

Gift Of Appreciation
For Your
Sponsorship
Seed of $100
or More
Gift Of Appreciation

My Gift Of Appreciation To My Sponsors!
...Those Who Sponsor One Square Foot In The Completion Of The Wisdom Center!

Thank you so much for becoming a part of this wonderful project...The completion of The Wisdom Center! The total purchase and renovation cost of this facility (10,000 square feet) is just over $1,000,000. This is approximately $100 per square foot. **The Wisdom Commentary is my Gift of Appreciation for your Sponsorship Seed of $100...that sponsors one square foot of The Wisdom Center. Become a Sponsor!** You will love this Volume 1, of The Wisdom Commentary. It is my exclusive Gift of Appreciation for The Wisdom Key Family who partners with me in the Work of God as a Sponsor.

Add 10% For S/H

H | **THE WISDOM CENTER** P.O. Box 99, Denton, Texas 76202 | **1-888-WISDOM1** **(1-888-947-3661)** | Website: WWW.THEWISDOMCENTER.TV